A Character Building Book™

Learning About Justice from the Life of
César Chávez

Jeanne Strazzabosco

The Rosen Publishing Group's
PowerKids Press™
New York

JB
Chavez S

Published in 1996 by The Rosen Publishing Group, Inc.
29 East 21st Street, New York, NY 10010

First Edition

Book design: Erin McKenna

Photo credits: Cover © Archive Photos; pp. 4, 7, 8, 12, 16 © AP/Wide World Photos; p. 11 © Cliff Hollenbeck/International Stock; p. 15 © Jonathan E. Pite/International Stock; p. 19 © Michele and Tom Grimm/International Stock; p. 21 © R. Bastone/Photoreporters.

Strazzabosco, Jeanne.
    Learning about justice from life of César Chávez / Jeanne Strazzabosco.
       p.   cm. — (A Character building book)
    Includes index.
    Summary: Examines the life of César Chávez, the Mexican American labor leader who achieved justice for migrant farm workers by creating a union to protect their rights.
    ISBN 0-8239-2417-3
    1. Chavez, Cesar, 1927–1993—Juvenile literature. 2. Labor leaders—United States—Biography—Juvenile literature. 3. Trade-unions—Migrant agricultural laborers—United States—Officials and employees—Biography—Juvenile literature. 4. Mexican Americans—Biography—Juvenile literature. 5. United Farm Workers—History—Juvenile literature. [1. Chavez, Cesar, 1927–1993. 2. Labor leaders. 3. Mexican Americans—Biography. 4. United Farm Workers—History. 5. Justice.] I. Title. II. Series.
HD6509.C48S77 1996
331.88'13'092   96-16091
                                              CIP
                                              AC

Manufactured in the United States of America

Table of Contents

Working on the Farm

César Estráda Chávez was born in Yuma, Arizona, in 1927. His grandfather had come to the United States from **Mexico** (MEK-sih-koh). He had started a farm. César's parents worked on the farm. They raised just enough food to eat. Because César's parents were Mexican, he was called Mexican American. When he was young, César saw that Mexicans and Mexican Americans were often treated unfairly by others. These others were **prejudiced** (PREH-juh-dist). César knew prejudice was wrong. Throughout his life, César worked for **justice** (JUS-tis).

◀ *César is a hero to many people, especially to Mexican Americans and to farmworkers.*

5

Losing the Farm

When César was 10 years old, his family lost their farm. It was during the Great Depression, a bad time for many people. Like César's family, many farmers didn't have enough money to be able to keep their farms.

Those farmers learned that they could earn money in California as **migrant** (MY-grent) farmworkers. Migrant farmworkers travel from farm to farm, picking vegetables, cotton, and fruit. César's family decided to go to California to become migrant farmworkers.

Migrant farmworkers pick all kinds of crops, including cherries. ▶

Life as a Migrant Worker

Migrant farmwork was hard. César and his family traveled all over California picking crops. Living conditions for farmworkers were bad. They often lived in a one-room shack with no running water or bathrooms. César's family spent the whole day in the fields picking vegetables. Their backs ached all the time. They were paid very little.

Unlike most workers in the United States, farmworkers were not protected by **labor** (LAY-ber) laws. They had no rights. Life was hard and frustrating.

◀ *Migrant farmworkers once had little control over their living or working conditions.*

9

Farmworkers' Fears

Like César's family, most migrant workers were Mexican or Mexican American. They had few skills other than farming. They relied on farm-work to support themselves and their families. Many workers didn't have the time or a way to learn English. They couldn't speak with their employers. So they couldn't ask for higher wages or better working conditions. Workers that could speak English didn't ask because they were afraid they would lose their jobs or be sent back to Mexico. Working conditions in Mexico were often even worse than on the U.S. farms.

Farm and vineyard owners often took advantage of migrant farmworkers. ▶

School

In the winter, there were few crops to be picked. César was able to go to school then. He was shy and too embarrassed to raise his hand. But he did listen. That was how he learned to speak English. Because his family moved so often, César kept changing schools. By eighth grade, César had gone to nearly 40 schools. On weekends and during vacations, César worked in the fields with his mom and dad.

Many children of migrant farmworkers help their parents pick crops during the summer, when school is out.

César as Teacher

Once César learned English, he could talk to the English-speaking field hands. He learned which farms paid the most money and which **cheated** (CHEE-tid) the workers. César told his parents and other farmworkers what he learned. At that time, most Mexican American farmworkers spoke only Spanish. César also taught others how to speak, read, and write English.

A few years later, César left his family and found work in vineyards picking grapes. He found that the workers there were also treated poorly. This injustice bothered him very much.

It made César angry that migrant farmworkers, such as this grape picker, were treated poorly. ▶

The CSO

One day, someone from a group called the Community Service Organization, or CSO, asked César to work with the group. The CSO taught César to help other farm-workers. César convinced Mexican Americans to **register** (REH-jis-ter) to vote. By voting, farmworkers could help change the way they were treated. César helped Mexicans become American **citizens** (SIT-ih-zenz). César knew farmworkers deserved fair pay and healthy working conditions.

◀ *Many people supported César's work, including the former Mayor of New York, David Dinkins.*

17

The UFW

César and his wife started the United Farm Workers **Union** (YOON-yun), or UFW. This was the first union for farmworkers. He went from farm to farm asking workers to join. Each family who joined paid a small amount of money to become a member. With that money, César did many things that helped farmworkers. He opened drugstores and grocery stores where workers could buy things for less money. He hired lawyers to help workers who were treated unfairly by their employers. The association even loaned money to members.

The rights of all farmworkers are protected by the UFW. ▶

Striking for Justice

In 1965, a group of grape pickers went on **strike** (STRYK). They asked for César's help. He and the UFW joined the strike. Grape pickers who were members of the UFW stopped picking. They demanded that the grape growers give them higher wages and better working conditions. People all across the country sent money, clothes, and food to the striking workers. César convinced Americans to **boycott** (BOY-kot) the vineyards by not buying grapes from California. César stopped eating until the strike ended. He didn't eat for 25 days.

◀ *César fought hard for justice for farmworkers. He won the battle.*

Justice for Farmworkers

In 1970, five years after the strike began, the grape growers finally gave in. They agreed to increase wages and make working conditions better. And U.S. labor laws were changed to protect the rights of farmworkers.

César Chávez died in 1993. But he is remembered for his fight for justice. He worked hard to improve farmworkers' living and working conditions. Through his efforts, farmworkers today have several unions that protect their rights.

Glossary

boycott (BOY-kot) Not buying or preventing others from buying something in protest.

cheat (CHEET) To do business in a way that is not fair or honest.

citizen (SIT-ih-zen) Member of a country.

justice (JUS-tis) Fairness.

labor (LAY-ber) Work.

Mexico (MEK-sih-koh) Country bordering the United States in Latin America.

migrant (MY-grent) Person who moves from place to place.

national (NAH-shun-ul) Belonging to a whole country, not just one area.

prejudice (PREH-juh-diss) An opinion formed without taking the time and care to judge fairly.

register (REH-jis-ter) To have your name on a list or record.

strike (STRYK) When workers refuse to work until their demands are met.

union (YOON-yun) Group of workers joined together to protect their rights.

Index

DATE			